TOMORROW'S LIVING ROOM

D1570671

May Swenson
Poetry Award Series

TOMORROW'S LIVING ROOM

poems
by

Jason Whitmarsh

UTAH STATE UNIVERSITY PRESS
Logan, Utah
2009

For Maeve —
The first, and
second-best,
of my books

All best —

Utah State University Press
Logan, Utah 84322–7200

www.usu.edu/usupress

Cover design by Barbara Yale-Read
Cover art: Megan Whitmarsh

Manufactured in the United States of America
Printed on recycled, acid-free paper

ISBN: 978-0-87421-746-9 (cloth)
ISBN: 978-0-87421-747-6 (paper)
ISBN: 978-0-87421-748-3 (e-book)

Library of Congress Cataloging-in-Publication Data

Whitmarsh, Jason.
  Tomorrow's living room : poems / by Jason Whitmarsh.
    p. cm. -- (May Swenson Poetry Award series)
  ISBN 978-0-87421-746-9 (cloth : alk. paper)
  I. Title.
  PS3623.H58548T66 2009
  811'.6--dc22
                                    2009009775

For Kerry

CONTENTS

FOREWORD

Tomorrow's Living Room is simply too good a collection of poems to allow me to indulge in the customary literary judge's protestations about how difficult it was to choose among so many excellent manuscripts. There were reading pleasures to be had along the way, and I fully enjoyed them, but the winner jumped out at me, as I hope it will for you, like a big bass breaking the surface of a lake after a long spell of staring at the water.

The poems speak for themselves, of course, but let me offer a word on their behalf.

We all appreciate a certain degree of clarity in the poems we read (don't we?), but we also like being blind-sided by abrupt shifts and turns we did not see coming. *Tomorrow's Living Room* is just such an exciting and accomplished mixture of directness and imaginative surprise. In paging through the manuscript, I found myself walking blithely into one poem after another, comforted by the casual, familiar tone of a colloquial voice only to find myself soon lost in a zone not of my own making—a stranger in Jason Whitmarsh's strange, alluring verbal land. Whenever I heard the door of tomorrow's living room clicking shut behind me, I knew I was in for some pleasurable disorientation.

These poems love getting off to a flying start. Many opening lines made me feel as if the poet and I had already been involved in an ongoing exchange to which I needed to pay more attention. "My stun gun no longer stuns much" one poem begins, striking a casual yet disturbing note. Another starts out by telling me "I don't mind the story you're telling, but can you please lean back in the chair and turn the light down." "What chair?" the logical part of me wants to ask, but the other part knows better. And there is no need to waste time establishing a setting when you can begin a poem with "I had the last undertaker in my pocket" or "Here we are in our lackluster hats."

Also keeping the reader on his or her toes is the mix of forms deployed by Whitmarsh, including prose poems, some standard quatrains, a one-line poem—there is even a clerihew for Dick Cheney. While taking advantage of the imaginative freedoms offered exclusively by poetry, these poems work carefully within chalk circles of limitation.

With so many poets working the American idiom these days, it is a wonder to find one with an original voice, but Jason Whitmarsh has carved out a verbal territory for himself unlike anyone else's. It is the kind of voice that whistles for our attention.

Billy Collins

ACKNOWLEDGMENTS

My thanks to the editors of the following magazines, in which some of these poems first appeared: *American Letters & Commentary, The Antioch Review, Denver Quarterly, Fence, The Harvard Review, Heat, Meanjin, New American Writing, Ploughshares, Verse,* and *The Yale Review.*

My gratitude and thanks to my children, Margaret, Henry, and Oliver; my parents; and my brothers and sisters. I'm particularly thankful to my mother, Dorothy, my sister, Megan, and my brother, Ian, for their contributions to these poems and to my life as a writer.

I'm also grateful to those friends and teachers who have helped with these poems, both directly and indirectly: Linda Bierds, Jeffrey Blomstrom, Eric McHenry, Heather McHugh, Catherine Wing, the Forgers' Circle, and, especially, Brian Henry and Richard Kenney.

Among his many other gifts, Cody Walker is a great friend and a great reader: Thank you.

Finally, my thanks to Kerry for her conversation, her laughter, and her love.

TOMORROW'S LIVING ROOM

FORECASTS

It might not happen, but if it does,
we'll be unhappy until it's over.
(When she switched from How could I
to Who did I think I, I kept thinking, Take cover.)

*

The rock fell from a great and far-off height
and plummeted silently through the roof
into bed, where it replaced your heart.
That's what I think. It's why you're so aloof.

*

There's a change when I come home,
like a queen batting her fake lashes
as she tells the jailer that today
it's forty, not twenty lashes.

*

The kids are watching television
while we ignore each other and the vision
of a young John the Baptist cursing
his future God. We'll fix things tomorrow, first thing.

HE SAID THESE THINGS,
NOT EVEN I COULD FORGIVE HIM

I'm kind of reluctant to mention the superhero powers
I've acquired since last we talked. It's probably best
that you don't focus on my biceps or the glow my skeleton makes
when you clang your fork against the plate. I'll tell you
what happened later. And don't say the word "Pilot,"
that does something special to my nervous system.
I'll tell you what happened before: In my dream
I grabbed an electric fence and when I woke I said
how strange to be in pain in a dream and you said
I was lucky it wasn't worse, those fences are dangerous.

OF ARC

It was the Era of Ostentatious.
Everywhere you went, the racket
lasted all night while machines fleshed out
the least of the world's mysteries.
Plain, as a category, had been dismissed.
Mirrors doubled what was left in sight:
Unsunk boats adrift on a lake, risk-
averse lovers apart in bed. Tonight,
you said, will be a simple affair,
but I, I wonder. What if behind
the curtain was only an after-
thought—an arcless moon, devoid of shine?
(You make out like there's nothing wrong,
you keep to that look of the looked-upon.)

ANNIVERSARY

This was a time when if it wasn't one thing, it was another. If you wanted a bike (I select here a random example; hundreds of others come to mind), it wasn't enough to go to a bike store and select a model. Certain formalities had to be observed, involving forms, lunch invitations, afternoon teas, and frequent phone conversations with an adviser, whose offer of help felt more sinister by the day. (Truth be told, buying a bike isn't even the most extreme example.) And the amount of bikes to choose from changed without notice, ranging from the vast—dozens of variations in handlebars, tires, and colors—to the miniscule, where two wheels and red paint was almost too much to ask. (Finding a wife, for example, was a whole order of difficulty beyond buying a bike. Perhaps that makes sense, though, considering that the bike, unlike the wife, was not also trying to find you, and thus filling out its own forms, fielding calls from its own advisers, and warily negotiating its own terms of engagement.)

DEPARTMENT STORE FICTIONS

The mannequins are all in love with you
and too depressed to say it. The cashier
flirts with another cashier, who eyes you,
who eyes the sales rack of wool pants.
Behind each mirror hunches an old man
watching women adjust their skirts,
their sunglasses, their hair. Small dogs disappear
on the escalator. Everyone leans forward
at the perfume counter, asking to be touched.

TOMORROW'S LIVING ROOM

My stun gun no longer stuns much. A few ants,
bits of people's fingers. And no one's sent
the new recording devices in some time now.
Our rewinders have been petitioning the restless;
our restless have been dangling their feet.
Their canyons need upkeep, their bogs
need tending. Otherwise the sick will be at your door,
too, wanting a vaccination against all that's wrong
with us, and them. Something in the debutante's
hand-me-downs had me thinking of you.
Her skirt was muddied from overplay, her list
of things to do not yet done today.

ONE ART

At ten, I wanted to be a kung fu master
like Bruce Lee, bare-chested, sideways, intent
on hitting my way out of disaster.

In the unmade and unimagined fluster
of being young, I hadn't yet spent
much time on *how* to be a kung fu master,

except to watch Lee get meaner, get faster.
He seemed genuinely pissed off, like he meant
to kill every actor, cause *real* disaster.

They attacked one by one (why?), and the last, or
next-to-last had knives and guns that went
nowhere. "You want some?" (Me, as kung fu master.)

That childhood is now both remote and vaster,
and Lee is a death and a continent
away. He'd already had his disaster

by the time I was watching every gesture—
his kicks, a flip, a scream. It's evident
why I wanted to be a kung fu master,
as though desire alone could prevent disaster.

TWO PARTS WATER

While Three stacks sand on the tide wall. The welcome wagon dropped them here, between tours of the mudflats, between old men lining up shots of birds on one leg. Two says, It's always been almost exactly like this, hasn't it?, and Three misses what a dozen of us couldn't fail to catch. The path across the flats is a false one; follow it and you end on a hill, severed from the other's horizon.

THE EVER INCONSTANCY

Everything's a prologue these days, One thinks. The music he hears, cornered in the elevator, keeps seeming about to burst into something else. The carpet about to run to tile or sandstone, the walls to ripple. The men next to him, in striped blue, hitting floor numbers, about to sing.

TWO, COUCHBOUND

Two's calculation of death over time: Ten thousand bodies a thousand years ago is five hundred bodies when Columbus lands, perplexed by the undergrowth, is one hundred when the railroad runs through, is ten when anyone you've known was born, is, this year, one. One comes home, briefcase in hand, sobbing.

AFTER ARCHILOCHOS

All of these horses are good,
and these horses, too,
and the ones you're hiding behind the wall,
I'll take those as well.

CHANGE

Change makes news
not with what's new
but by pulling
what's lost into view.
This man today
has another man's face.
Something must
have taken him
or taken place.

MISSING IOU

Eve's Scene

Eve's secret dessert ended
her flesh-dress, fenced Eden,
sentenced her descendents—
even rejected G-d, her best defender.
Next week? Endless Hell: The Descent.

Adam's Act

Adam's a bad-ass card shark, man.
Talks back, acts all alpha, calls a bat a bat,
a banana a banana, has a karma alarm.
Man's a class act. Can an asp charm Adam?
Ask G-d: "Draw a card, Adam—draw a straw.
A last straw." Adam falls fast, falls far.

CURSE

A life like mine, but without the happy bits,
or a life like yours, but without the money,
the success, the admiration of your peers,
the several European awards, the looks, the wit,
the economy and grace of motion, the talent.

JAPANESE WATERMELON

Obama v. Hillary is better than Bush and better, too, than popping your small head into a square jar and growing it into a box, which is also better than Bush, but you're getting closer.

ADMINISTRATION

Richard B. Cheney
is considered brainy
because, Christ, what else is there?
A chest of old bones and foul air?

*

The latest president
set a precedent
for torture, election stealing, and lying your way into war.
(He'd been told that that's what being president was for.)

THREE DAYS IN
AND ALREADY IT'S COME TO THIS

Others were at it, too, absolving anyone
they could think of of anything they did.
Meanwhile, the same as always: Talkies
on the television screen and black-and-white photos
in the galleries. Shrimp cocktails for lunch,
maybe later a coffee and someone's telephone
ringing two rooms over. People think when you say
"I'm going to kill that motherfucker" you mean
something by it, that's all I'm saying.

FASTED AND LOOSED

That the saddest trick in the world involves
saws and cufflinks and a one-legged bird
most people already know, but rarely does
anyone ask the right question afterward.
Even so, it takes a while to remember
who last saw the pigeon, flying lopsided
toward a dense forest, in her wings the fresh flowers
and the feathers and the hollow pigeon bones,
of course, and the muscles that move them.
One takes no notice of the sky,
how wet it's become, or the sun, how it's all
but disappeared. The trees, by the rocks' reckoning,
are recently planted, the people always leaving.

TRIOLET

Here we are in our lackluster hats,
at your door and wanting it, too.
Mind the doormen, mind the old bats,
here they are in their lackluster hats,
walking their jewels, and all unattached.
Here's our good time, spent by me, spent on you,
here we are in our lackluster hats,
at your door and wanting it, too.

ANNIVERSARY

Happiness is on display in a downtown gallery. He wants to go see it; she says they haven't the time, and besides, it's certain not to be any good. "We're not New York. All they show here are watercolors and stained glass." It's been getting great reviews, happiness has. Galleries in other cities have made offers. Perhaps more could be made, or, if not, this happiness could be moved. You'd have to think it through, first, the danger of taking something like that elsewhere. It might not survive, or it might survive so well that the original would seem a trick. It could keep you up at night, protecting happiness.

CAPITALISM AS COMEUPPANCE

Alternate Tuesdays he   tolls in the office
with the modest manners   of the metered at work.
Why not withered?   —and worn from lunches
of saltlicks and sandbars   in the sunlit cafe,
the breath a capstone   of bright fatigue
and the elevator   vanishing at five
a trick of the light.   It's labeled unfit
and filed in the drawer   by "fever-pitched,"
near the quartered starts   of the quieted few,
even their torture not their own.   The tic of the eye
becomes all the talk: how terrible, they say,
how terrible that we   in the towers and visions
whistle no longer   and still watch the clock.

So much to go on, they said, but no sooner
had we crafted a sentiment than the world
would off and disappear on us.
It was that eerie over-the-shoulder appraisal
that had us in cahoots with the wrong sort,
that had us running from the news of the day.
Those are just placards, you know—a dullard's gift
to another, less dull, dullard. This hall of mirrors
has me looking so fat, so old—tell me, did
all the Miseries choose my skeleton to hang
their hats on? Even when a bailiff is cornered,
his cousins come after you, telephones raised.

REGRET

Unlike the other porcupines, this one is all trouble all the time. His bruising antics have called into question the having of a porcupine at all. At the end of the porcupine is a feast. The knives will have been sharpened, the table set with the fluted spoons, the guests invited. They will have arrived with wide throats and make terrible noises as they descend. The porcupine will have trembled.

PRAISE

It never rises to
the occasion, never replaces
its opposite. You can't
exchange it for goods,
can't store it as
something to have when
lost at sea. It's
inaccurate (for one thing),
hitting the spot you
thought you'd left behind.
And any pleasure ends
before it does—like
someone looking away
while you finish the joke.
(If only he knew
of what he spoke.)

She was a wicked woman, but not so you could tell. Many people thought of her as good, as good as anyone they knew. When they told her as much, she smiled and shook her head and so seemed to them humble, and so even more good. But meanwhile her leg clattered up and down like a nyloned piston and her fingers drummed the underneath of the table, all of which I saw and heard from the floor where I slept.

THERE'S AN OLD MAN

There's an old man that washes out the country pool twice an afternoon three times a week and he's a funny old man he told me a story once about how he almost drowned and afterwards we laughed and laughed as though his twin brother hadn't actually drowned when he almost drowned, which his brother had and which he hadn't. There's sometimes when the old man calls me on the phone this is late at night and I answer and there's no sound at first and I think well it's either the old man or his dead drowned twin brother and either way it's probably going to be funny.

NOT A DEMON

Some insist that anything
that makes us less hell-bent
is money well-spent,
but you have to wonder
if the theory those acts depend on
is what we want our souls trained on.
Better, maybe, to let the guilt metastasize
than to cancel by good intent
any chance to surprise.

AND QUARTERED

After the scare in the nursery, everyone stopped
taking their jasmine for granted. Even forsythia
seemed more vibrant, more worth a stop and stare.

Amidst rumors of media, they carted the lovers
out a side door, belts and shoelaces removed.
In some prisons, one said, they dress you in paper.

The gurney rattled across the town's new asphalt.
The media, a single helicopter, made no landing.
The wind tore the shirts from the crowd.

ANNIVERSARY

We were charged with either the correcting or protecting of someone. (We couldn't hear well when the instructions were given.) Sometimes they're one and the same, as when you stop a boy from running into the street, or caution him not to throw knives into the air. We'd rather these sometimes were the only times, that all correction was protection. We'd rather this was well understood. He fakes something dangerous and watches us flinch. The rain continues.

10: Abduction

The lion trap has caught a bird,
three messengers, and the twins
from the orphanage. So far, no lion.

11: Daring Enterprise

"For the betterment of science, or man"
worked not at all, so they tried story B—
"it's an adventure, undertaken for
the purpose of obtaining a woman"—
which, with a few changes, got
the monkey into the aluminized gloves,
treated canvas and rubber stockings,
and automated parachute, made of
white nylon and seeming, when spilled, to shift
and close in a way not entirely unlike
their beloved, and he understood then
that this nearness too was a kind of joy,
and meant to ask the surrounding voices
if all desires were given women's names,
but by this time the countdown had begun.

31: Imprudent Rivalry with a Deity

"So I said to Him, you want
a piece of me, man?"

THE THIRTY-SIX DRAMATIC SITUATIONS

1–36

His failed suicide was to avenge his sister, whom he killed by mistake while kidnapping his wife. The voices, speaking in code, had said she was ambitious—that she betrayed him, that he should find her, and tie her up, and ransom her for God.

Ever since, the family has kind of hated him.

ON THE TAKE

I had the last undertaker in my pocket.
He owed more than one can make
undertaking, and had agreed, in principle,
to a sort of indentured servitude.

*

Nine times out of ten, someone says
you have the last of something
and you don't, really. Just the second-to-last,
or it's unique this side of the ocean,
but in China every younger sister is wearing one.

*

The last undertaker? In my pocket.
He had that problem where the teeth
rattle and the stones stick to the flesh.

*

The undertaker's to-do list:
Wear black on Sunday.
Empty the gazebo in the rain.
Bury the dead.

ANNIVERSARY

She was nicest when he collapsed, but only when she thought he had really collapsed, and not fake-collapsed in order for her to be nice. Sometimes he fake-collapsed and she fell for it: she was nice. Sometimes he really collapsed and she thought it was fake, she didn't even ask him how he was doing. If she had asked (even pretended to ask, without wanting the answer), maybe he might've felt better, maybe he might've answered. She hands him the baby and says, Quick, let's go, we're late.

Croquet had cost him the family fortune
and much else besides. His thought now
was to grow flowers and sullen,
one on the heels of the other.
That his backyard had double-crossed him
in serious, uncompromising ways
seemed someone else's memory
as the season drew to a close—why not overlook
those few missed wickets, the untapped stakes?
Still, he kept towing the gargoyle statuary home.
They leered at the flamingos, coughed their drinks
into bird baths, and slept as fish are thought to,
eyes open. They dropped the whole neighborhood
into a new set of actuarial tables. His thought now
was to leave them to everything,
beyond which he hoped to journey
and report, midwinter, on the sights.

First, failure, misery, and death. For me,
but mostly for my children. Losing you,
or any variation on that theme.
Keeping you only by enclosing you
in pity and despair, or risks thereof.
Public speaking, outer space, slow flies,
balloons. Not knowing what I'm thinking of.
Old men in navy-blue, repeating lies.
Next, sitting here with less and less to say
as the hours quicken. Spinning the hearsay,
rewinding facts, unspooling opinion.
What's worth, within me, keeping an eye on?
The doubt, the shame, the muted "I sing"?
All duly noted, all unsurprising.

HE DREAMS OF THE DINER OF THE DAMNED

Everyone in the place
is eating something
you can't find on the menu.

*

The two-ninety-five special
takes forever to arrive, literally,
and when it does the toast is wheat, not white.

*

"What did you expect, chicken eggs?"

APOLOGY

That last love poem I gave you, I want to apologize for that. It was crudely put and several of the metaphors leaned too heavily on sea life. I love you so much more than that. The best part of the poem was the beginning, and that had nothing to do with you, or me, or how much either of us loves each other. It was just a line from another, better poem. Most of the poem sounds defensive, like I've been accused of not loving you, or you of not loving me. Not that I think I don't love you, or you me. I don't. Still, one could read a poem by someone else and it'd seem more authentic—you'd be more likely to think that poem was dedicated to you, I mean, than to think mine was. One could even argue, too, that by studiously avoiding your name or any identifying traits, I was making this poem fit for more than one person, like women in general, or a second wife, or your very attractive sister.

TWENTY QUESTIONS, THE ADVANCED EDITION

"Is it retromingent?"

SELF-PORTRAIT

I am sourly lit,
an ashcan emptied
and adrift, a split rock,
a hovering cloud
made dark and small
with age. The corner
of the yellow kitchen,
all grease and spilled wine,
the muddy footprints,
that's me and those are mine.
I am lifted as dead weight
and dropped in the damp,
the hole has me, the sides
have me, the rain started
as sunlight, the tricky bastard.

ANNIVERSARY

I'll take you apart and assemble a new one out of you, someone sweeter and with smaller hands and more to say. Miniature, almost, almost fit for a helium balloon to lift and send off. The parts left over can be another you, the you with the blank eyes and the bitter taste in the mouth. And this one I'll take up and this one I'll take down.

SONNET

What he can't name she sees in him always:
the compliments he rains on his own head
(sarcastically said, yes, but still, still said),
the good stories he guts, the way he strays
from tone to tone without much meaning to.
While driving home, they barely speak. He tries—
he watches, he avoids the obvious lies,
he thinks (but won't say), I've nothing for you.

Over this, she feels a kind—or kind of—
acceptance, though her friends are better now
(for her) and she's happiest while he's away.
Over this? He doesn't know, or can't say.
At least, she thinks, he must see, slightly, how
impossible those first words were. "My love—"

WHAT WE SAID THEN, THAT WASN'T NICE

Everyone here is white with grief.
(The madman, the butcher, the thief.)
Arrive early, or late as hell,
and wear the stuff that doesn't smell.
Make yourself up and take a drink
and tell us, dear, what's swell to think
about when the ground just gave way
beneath the lie of a summer day,
and the rot's got him and the rats
have her and yes, yes, of course, nat-
urally, I'd say I love you, just you,
but God knows who I'd be saying it to.

ANNIVERSARY

After the self-help seminar, he keeps adding the phrase "as a success-ful person" to his sentences. As a successful person, I feel like watch-ing TV tonight. As a successful person, can you help me wire the bathroom? He feels about 14% better, which, as a successful person, is a lot. What do you do in the face of real tragedy? she says. What phrase protects us from old age, from death, from the world and its empty spaces? As a successful person, I have no idea. It is the softest of boundaries, his spell, in constant motion, a barely wrought surface at all times surrounding him and, now that he thinks of it, her, too.

WHY POETRY? BECAUSE

I can't write a novel, said the raised hand.
I'm too dramatic, it takes lots of work,
my characters all talk the same (because
they're all a take on the same kind of jerk).

I've no idea why Jack in Chapter One
would still want Jill in Chapter Nine, nor what
it means to "indicate a quicker wit."
I'd be depressed by now if I'd started yet.

I think it's better to stick to what I know,
which is me, or the parts I've seen so far.
(Stick, too, to what keeps the evenings free,
or, if not, can be written in a bar.)

DEAR MORBID IN MALAYSIA
all lines from Dear Abby columns

Your suggestion will benefit not only mail carriers,
but all individuals with outdoor mailboxes.
The woman you have loved for five years appears
to have made her choice—it's Daddy, not you.

But all individuals with outdoor mailboxes
consult an attorney before assuming their union is legal.
To have made her choice—it's Daddy, not you—
in the atmosphere you describe is not healthy:

consult an attorney before assuming their union is legal.
You should know that a condom for women was invented years ago,
in an atmosphere I'd describe as unhealthy.
Treat its lifesaving devices with the respect they deserve.

You should (knowing that a condom for women was invented years ago)
try to get a dialog going so you can get inside his head.
Treat its lifesaving devices with the respect they deserve,
and send Velma a bunch of carrots, and tell her you're sorry.

Try to get a dialog going so you can get inside his head.
Talk in money-syllables. Say, "Thanks, but I'm not interested."
Send Velma a bunch of carrots, and tell her you're sorry.
You could be about seventeen years too late.

You don't live in Schenectady—you live in Atlanta,
where the woman you have loved for five years appears,
saying, "You have written an important letter. I'm printing it.
Your suggestion will benefit not only mail carriers, but us all."

THREE CURSES

The newspaper's been read, the cat drowned.
I wish you were still around.

*

Another minute with you.
Another minute without you.

*

Everything weak in us survives. It's meant to.
If not, not a day would go by where I'd want you.

ANNIVERSARY

He says, OK, I'm exactly who I am but this one thing is different—I don't have a nose, or don't know the word for table, or I sing with perfect pitch, but all the time—and do you still stay with me? and she says, But do you do this or have this? (No, I'm the same, I told you), or she says nothing, or she hears only the question not the setup and repeats it to herself and pauses, both of them hanging on the answer, and him with no nose.

LAST BIT

Everywhere I go
Is arranged just so.
The silver, the linens,
The late-night poker winnings.

Which is why finding you
Was such a bolt-from-the-blue.
Especially the you you've become:
Unhappy, old, stooped. Numb.

NIGHTMARE

Our son at night is scared not of the dark,
nor of the closet with its vast unseen
collection of unhappy monsters, green
and blue and damp and slung from every hook,
their eyes aglow and oddly numbered, stuck
on stalks or tentacles or (worst of all)
held in the hand and rolled across the hall,
where they close in for a closer look.
Of course, I'd rather him be terrified
of them than scared of what does keep him up:
our front-seat attacks, our bedridden fights,
our blank, scarred days. Better monsters than that.
(And he's asleep by the time we've been kind,
for which let's blame the dark, or him, or the wine.)

THE STORY YOU'RE TELLING

I don't mind the story you're telling, but can you please lean back in the chair and turn the light down. Can you talk more quietly. Can the neighbors leave their porch and go inside. The orchids behind you, can we rearrange them. Are you particular about the wine we drink while we listen. Have you given any thought to an ending and whether you'd like to be sitting or standing when it comes.

WE'RE A RERUN

We're a rerun, a couple of old hags
at it again on the back porch,
a green hospital wall, the conversion
of no one, we're a habit-forming substance
that is no longer regulated, a donation
to someone's sister's best friend's
run-down church, we're the day after,
we're delayed by a stutter, barked up,
backed into, belonging to each other
and (this gets worse with age)
no one else.

I THOUGHT THAT

What I forgot was equal to what I didn't know.
The capital of Paraguay and what I said that made you go.
The two, by my theory, weigh the same,
like any mistake you can or cannot name.

FAITH

It is unlikely that we will see you
today, as most of us have passed on

into sleep, or dinner, or that thing
we do with our thumb and forefinger

when each of us is looking the other
in the eye. So to speak. It is also unlikely

that we will see you tomorrow, which is cause
for no celebration but perhaps a drink—wine

would be proper, I suppose. Let me first open
the appointment book and register

your disappointment over our failure
to meet—what's the term?—our limits. Of course,

I could turn the entire thing over to you, and ask
what trust we should place in one so convinced

that by a series of endless decisions
we will arrive somewhere, find the milk

heating on the stove, the newspaper hanging
from the dog's mouth, all distant spaces

no longer in retreat. Watch this—you see?
Double joints let us do that.

ANNIVERSARY

We number our fights and say the numbers instead of saying the words. "Two," she says. "Fourteen, fourteen, fourteen." "I don't see how that's relevant," she says. "Irrelevant statements—isn't that twenty?" She stares a short while out the window, maybe because I'm winning. You can only see the rain by looking at what is already water on the ground. Other than this, the day looks clear. She's thinking of a number. I have one, too, a number and a packed bag and the children to think of.

GHAZAL

Sailors point out to sea, as if there were wisdom in the distance.
They've no idea, though—is it flotsam or jetsam in the distance?

One party says to the other, "Our phones are tapped.
The world's a place to fear. You can hear the hum, in the distance."

Complaining of neck pain, the general admires the view
from his hospital room. Are those candelabrums in the distance?

That night, night fell. Pages turned themselves in, libraries Deweyed
their bindings. Our letters rose like a column in the distance.

We lied when we said we walked the moor with no jacket,
a thin pair of shoes: No one really saw a golem in the distance.

Patients leave ladders at windows, their sheets tied to bedposts,
though the doctor swears there's no lack of symptoms in the distance.

To know a clock, keep time. To know a man, sleep late, as he does.
Accept as little, defer as much. Read his poem, "In the Distance."

HAVING AT IT

(Note: to rend, tear the limbs with great and unusual force.
To drone, enter into conversation with what is left.)

Return hangdog after twenty years, your hands empty or, worse, missing.
None rotted in that shade, but few, if any, thought to flourish.

Pick up a consolation prize on your way out—a miniature
Do Not Enter sign, a wooden plane. Someone's doll's face.

One begins ever after and ends upon a time. One swallows a knight.
Torn ode? Tenuous, you mean? Something less than a grammar of deceit?

PERFECT FORECASTING, FOUND ON EBAY

"It looks like it is or will be an antique."

FINNISH RABBIT

Everything past this point is going to matter,
but less terribly than it did before.

The same adventurers will suffer, but fewer
among their family will learn the sad truth,

and those that do will be told more gently,
with a solid squeezing of the shoulder

or a lingering stare into the eye, which by itself
can seem scary and inappropriate, but when matched

with a sincere tone occludes all sorts of hideous nonsense.
It's the blinking that has got us down.

That, and the fables about the bear and the children,
the way they keep taunting him and taunting him

and never get eaten.

ANNIVERSARY

She says he isn't as funny as he used to be. About fifty percent as funny, maybe less. He thinks, but doesn't say, no, it's you, you're depressed, you don't find anyone funny anymore. She thinks, but doesn't say, I've always been depressed. I've never found anyone funny—except you, once.

DISAPPEARING ACT

As the milkmaids do it, with aplomb—no ersatz,
beyond-the-fray attitude. The less you say
concerning my obsession with wax,
debutantes, and martinis, the better. How
else am I to make an impression? Even Pavlov
found his dogs to be a bit exaggerated. Like you:
good looking, maybe, but gimpy. A minor balloonist
hovers nearby, biding his time. He says rise, but you hear loss;
invention, and you strap wings to the projector,
jury-rigged with wire and plaster. You say your IQ
keeps climbing. You say, let's build a three-legged trap,
lift it into place on pulleys and gears, and catch so-and-so
making love to the wife. You never sleep past ten.
Not a man's at your beck and call but you lose him—
ordinary fellows, all, with wingtips and snapped hearts. They scowl,
pout, or take up hobbies; most must learn to drink.
Quietly, the balloonist descends, his declared raj
raining brimstone on the sand, sundering the cacti,
stripping oases of shade and water. He wanted too much
to begin with; they dared not repeat it. (No one knew anything
unusual about anyone else, even with the lights off.)
Viewing times are on the even hours. The shutter's in place:
Watch for the second entrance, the tousled bed
(X-ray detective work on an unhappy public).
You've heard, then, the week's forecast? Sub-
zero temperatures, no lines at the Cinerama.

ABOUT THE AUTHOR

Jason Whitmarsh received a B.A. in mathematics from the University of Chicago and an M.F.A. in poetry from the University of Washington. His poems have appeared in a number of journals, including *American Letters & Commentary, Denver Quarterly, Fence, The Harvard Review, New American Writing, Ploughshares, Verse,* and *The Yale Review.* He lives in Seattle with his wife and children. *Tomorrow's Living Room* is his first book.

THE MAY SWENSON POETRY AWARD

This annual competition, named for May Swenson, honors her as one of America's most provocative and vital writers. In John Hollander's words, she was "one of our few unquestionably major poets." During her long career, May was loved and praised by writers from virtually every major school of poetry. She left a legacy of nearly fifty years of writing when she died in 1989. She is buried in Logan, Utah, her birthplace and hometown.